ISBN: 9780578778358

BOOK CATEGORIES: POETRY

TABLE OF CONTENTS

An Intense Longing To Be Published

I just want to see my writings in print

Let the readers feel what my heart was feeling

as my pen took a sprint

Other writers know the intense longing that I have

to get my writings out there

This deep desire to get published

is something we all share

I know that there are so many people

that can feel what I've wrote

Ten years as a writer and often I still get

an editor's rejection note

They keep telling me that I need to make

this and that revision

If I were to do that then my story

would lose all of its precision

Maybe I'm too stubborn because I'm not willing

to compromise mine

I'll admit that there are a few sections

that I'll need to refine

Nobody seems to understand my intense desire

to see my writings between a book spine

The readers will feel me even before they read

between the line

Every publishing house that I go to,

I am faced with numerous sentries

So many middlemen tackling me

before I touch down to the main entries

These people are blind to what the public really

wants and needs

Corporate monopolies don't care

that I got mouths to feed

The years that I've been dreaming of getting published

is going on twelve

I am tired of these snobby editors who only

think of themselves

They turn down my quality work

and then turn around and put out this rubbish

My only solution is to be independent and self-publish

AT FIRST NOBODY FELT THE PASSION
OF THE DREAMER UNTIL

When he first told people about his dream,

they thought he couldn't do it

It was their aid that he first tried to solicit

So he went back to the drawing board

and started from scratch

Many critics doubted his vision,

but his passion he refused to let anyone snatch

This man just kept dreaming against all odds

Every time he asked for assistance,

they shook their head with negative nods

In spite of all this he didn't give up on his dream

The naysayers were loud in their opposition,

but his faith remained supreme

He had to keep forging ahead in the face of opposition
Never allowing doubt to creep in because a strong
belief system was his intuition
Still he knew he had to move on and keep going

Yeah there were many people who didn't believe
His dreams were too great
for their small minds to conceive
Over time he began to knock down the barriers
that stood in his way
He gained the assistance of people
who first told him nay

His passion began to spread to others
who surrounded him
A glow shined from his exterior
in a place that was once dim
He accomplished his dreams and did what others
couldn't do when they fell
At first nobody felt the passion of the dreamer until…

ALL I EVER WANTED TO DO WAS BE SOMEBODY

All my life all I ever wanted to do was be somebody

No one that I know wants to be a nobody

Everyone wants to amount to more than nothing

If they say they don't, I believe they are bluffing

When you have a body that is,

you have to find something more to live for

The only way to do that is go deep inside

your spiritual core

Most of us just live on the surface

and don't go beyond that

We block spirituality from getting in

when it steps on our doormat

I always wanted to be important in somebody's eyes

As a youngster I stayed in trouble

and was one of the bad guys

Maturity taught me that I had to find a deeper purpose

In some way we can all find our own story

written in these verses

I know the readers feel this because all they ever
wanted to do was be somebody also
We want our life to be colorful like the gecko
Throughout this short life,
I have had so many dreams of making it big
Strong like the redwood tree
So adversity couldn't break my will like a twig

I may not be that important somebody yet,
But I'm striving to be that person
When my encore comes, I'll own that stage
without any rehearsing

I had a lot of practice
because being something important
Is the notion that travels through my body
It's been this way my whole life in that
All I ever wanted to do was be somebody

THE COLD OF TODAY

When I speak of the cold,

I'm not only speaking of the weather

This is about chilling winds

that can't be covered up with a sweater

As I write these words,

starving children will die of malnutrition overnight

When we go outside to protest these injustices

we will catch the frostbite

Bitten by the winds from the sneeze of a rich tyrant

Sending us into certain refuge like a migrant

Never far from your mind is the impoverished people

Who don't even have a window

Their lack of shelter from the cold is as harsh as

an arrow shooting from a bow

When it feels like this, it has to be below zero

Bundle up with divine protection

before stepping out of your door

This bitter cold has put somber on your persona

Now we do all that we can not to catch pneumonia

Mighty are the economic winds that blow down

shelter for the poor

Exposing the elements of greedy institutions

all the way down to the core

It's so cold today, but yet I remain hopeful

of a warmer tomorrow

A sun that will shine some light through

the darkness of this sorrow

Until then we have to cover and try to stay warm

Helping those in need find shelter in the storm

Along the path of life, I search for comfort,

But get cold shoulders along the way

It's so cold outside today

MEMORIES ARE VISITS

When you have a memory of an event,

it is like going to that place all over again

So vivid in how it replays in your mind

like a duplicate twin

In your head you see it so clear

You feel like déjà vu must be near

Deep inside your brain cells

is where these memories reside

By the laws of nature when you recall them,

they abide

You concentrate on them and they become your focus

Even bringing to your attention things at first

that you didn't notice

In our limited capacity,

memories are how we time travel

Going down old roads where concrete

has replaced the gravel

Times long gone by that we forgot about

begins to illuminate

Putting these events into context

and bringing them back up to date

We have a brain that was constructed for observation

Accurately filing each memory

safely without any negation

All of life's experiences is in the repository of the mind

Some of them we have blocked out

and never want to find

There are a lot of things that we would like to forget

We survived these incidents

and would like to get over it

Sometimes thing come to us in pieces and bits

Reminding us of the past because memories are visit

<u>A Common Kindred Among The Working Class</u>

Among the working class there is a certain kindred

The way that they make do with,

so little is very splendid

Understanding each other's plight allows them

to deal with others in compassion

Wearing the honor of being the working class

on their sleeve is strong a statement of fashion

It is their labor that pays the taxes

and keeps the economy afloat

Without such efforts the inflation rate will bloat

Therefore, their place in society

should not be underestimated

The corporate bosses need to realize this

when worker's pay is deflated

In the trenches of a factory,

they mass produce the goods we consume

All the things we use everyday from food to perfume

The workers are concerned
about our health and sage quality
Greedy corporations multiply profits by cranking out
volume that reduces quality

The working class relates to each other because
they are in the same struggle
They must continue to fight for their rights
and with the bosses they can't snuggle
Finding solace and comfort within their own ranks
When it comes to empty spaces in the economy,
they fill in the blanks

Kindred because they are related
by the most common seed
Taking care of their family
and fulfilling a universal need
Together they are a united mass
Displaying the common kindred
among the working class

Cosmic Truth

Look at the heavens and all you see is cosmic truth

Peep through your telescope,

but be prepared to spend hours in the booth

High powered equipment to verify your findings,

But outside the earth's stratosphere there is no lie

Just endless galaxies that can't be seen

with the naked eye

Heavenly bodies orbiting to a pre-ordained law

Putting men in amazement at what they saw

Sending him back to study in his laboratory

Now he has to modify his theory and change

the entire scientific story

Cosmic truth is the same today

as it was in ancient times

It was only some bygone galaxies

that died off in their primes

The universe as a whole was never comatose

An eclipse is when some parts

of the earth are overshadowed

By darkness like a ghost

Everything outside of the earth's hemisphere is cosmic

We get a piece of that world when a meteorite crashes

into the earth in the form of a brick

Mankind is in search of answers,

so we follow wherever our leader goes

I know that what we are looking for is somewhere

out there in the cosmos

Stare out into space and you will see that the universe

is constantly expanding

The stars orbiting their planets are ever demanding

When stars die, they are digested into their galaxy

without getting chewed by not one of its tooth

Even if we question what the scientists tell us,

we should never doubt cosmic truth

Poets Of Change

I am in the class of the poets of change
Writing for a serious purpose and not just to entertain
We have a deep passion for the words of change
that our writings express
The readers can feel the urgency in our address

Throughout history it was words that inspired people
to make the changes that needed to be made
If it is said or wrote correctly, it can cut through
obstacles and doubts with the force of a blade
Words contain power,
but we just have to use them in the right way
That's why poets of change need to be careful
in what we say

Every human being uses words

to get their point across

We just write it down,

so the substance of the words don't get lost

Poets trying to change the world

because we believe in the power of what we write

Our main agenda is to better this world's plight

A change is coming, but we must be ready for it

In our lives change must always have a place to fit

When it does come, we have to be able to adjust

Never hatching all of our eggs in one nest

Evolution is in a constant state of progress

As the world evolves

its inhabitants are under so much stress

Even while you are reading this, millions of people are

starving from a hunger pang

We hope that the readers of our writings will aid them

because we are poets of change

It Ain't A Pretty Picture

Have you ever seen a picture

that was hard to understand

It leaves you to wonder what was wrong

with the painter's hand

Well this picture is a reflection of my troubled life

I grew up in extreme poverty surrounded by

heartache and strife

If my life story were a picture

It would be like reading from hell's scripture

With the pages burning at your eyes

poking with the fiery

of a scorching pitchfork

Tears filled with flames is the only light

on a path that is so dark

Look at this picture and take this journey with me

Frame your thoughts with empathy

as you view this harsh reality

It hurts me when I see it so I know it might hurt you

Behold let me reveal this portrait without further ado

The picture is scary when you first see it

Then your vision absorbs each color bit by bit

Through the maze appears a boy who is hurt and lost

Trapped in a cold world with a warm heart

not embittered by the frost

On his face is a question asking why he is hungry

He is surrounded by family, yet he feels so lonely

Imagining changing the world and wishing he wasn't

so poor was his favorite hobby

This picture is a story about the life

of a child named Bobby

The reflection in this boy's eye is that of pain

There wasn't much time for playing

because he had to work to stay sane

His eyes say that he wants to be saved

The streets he walks down are full of glass

and the roads are not paved

Raw Material

So much can be created out of raw material

Especially when the quality of the product is imperial

You can craft it in your own mold

A unique creation in which you

have ownership rights to hold

The material is raw,

but you blend it all together to get the right mix

Breaking the components down to their finest

mathematical fix

The finished product was made from

everything organic

In the beginning stages of trial and error,

You served as the mechanic

When you bundle raw material up

it gets all combusted and compact

After you release it into the air nature starts to react

Through these various processes, one element

takes on a dominate trait

Its own weaker characteristics it begins to annihilate

A writer, builder, or a scientist

all need raw material to build

That's how a craftsman first begins

to experiment in their field

From experiment to firsthand experience

emerges the finished product

Once it is final it's complete

and there's nothing else to deduct

In all of the natural compounds of the universe

I see a potential creation

Raw material but when you put it together

it comes alive like animation

There is no violation because you are still

In harmony with natural law

Combining the elements of nature

using material that is raw

R   A   W

E   U   R

A   T   I

L   E   T

      N   E

      T   R

      I

      C

Using The Wisdom Of An Adage

In my poems I often use the wisdom of an adage

At times even using them as my title page

There's just something special about an old saying

That's why many phrases come and go,

but these have the power of staying

Old sayings from centuries ago still get casual mention

When we hear these things, we take notice

and pay close attention

There is a lot of wisdom in these words

They stand out individually and don't run in herds

Often these adages are prophetic

Tune into the message because it's phonetic

Most of these sayings come from ordinary people

and not the mystics

Yet they are all so full of knowledge,

You'd think they came from a Master of Physics

Just a few words but they contain so much meaning

These are the type of phrases that make you

want to do some soul cleaning

Short messages but so long in their reach

The way these words were constructed

is designed to teach

When I talk or write I'll use an adage

to drive my point home

Going inside the rooms of your mind to settle

where the concentration doesn't roam

I try to give constructive criticism to myself and others

without much ego bruising

In situations like this, it will be the wisdom

of an adage that I'll be using

WE ALWAYS TELL OURSELVES WHAT WE CAN'T DO

Quite often people give up and tell themselves

what they can't do

Without even putting forth a harder effort,

They're convinced that this is true

Some people don't even realize their own strength

They give up before going the whole length

Things can be so simple, but we make it so complex

Our bodies are equipped to finish the task

With a built-in survival reflex

When it seems that we can't go on,

we must continue to proceed

Challenging ourselves to complete the deed

As long as we tell ourselves we can't do it,

then that's what we'll believe

Instead of struggling harder,

we'll excuse ourselves with a reprieve

Man always wants to go the easy route

That's not what winning a hard-earned

victory is about

No matter how hard it might be, you must complete

that project that comes up next

Don't tell yourself that you can't do it

under a false pretext

You can do it as long as you persevere

Rise above your failure while overcoming your fear

If you give up it's only yourself that you shortchange

On your shoulder is where the responsibility will hang

The art of life is the frame and giving up is not

the picture we should paint

This is exactly what will happen if we keep

telling ourselves that we can't

BLANK CANVASES

Looking at blank canvases with visions

of so much that could be there

Eyeing the scene picturing beautiful manifestations

of art everywhere

Now the canvases are no longer blank

My mind just painted a portrait of a treasure chest

Made of wooden plank

If you had a blank canvas, what would you paint

Would your art portray a villain or a saint

When people observe pictures,

they interpret them in different ways

One observer may see a labyrinth,

whereas someone else may describe it as a maze

Our minds are like a canvas

that we constantly paint on

Drawing life as it appears in our mental zone

Some paint a happy scene, while others signal distress

Calling our attention to the plight of these

who have less

The face in the picture has a faraway look

Your mind has to imagine their story

because it isn't told in a book

Look closer at the eyes,

you might see something that you recognize

You cannot ignore their suffering is what you realize

Distant galaxies are like blank canvases,

waiting on a cosmic

even to draw their conclusion

Swimming in the cosmos with particles

combined as cosmic fusion

Imagine space as a blank canvas awaiting your artistic

creation to give it definition

Draw the picture clearly

as you are guided by your intuition

FUNERAL: INTO A LIFE WITHOUT THAT PERSON

At a funeral we anticipate how life will be

without a person that we know

Crying as a result of memories from long ago

How can we make it through life without them

It will be like putting on our once favorite hat

without the brim

One person can change life for everyone

whom they've ever met

Other people inspire the minds of people who

haven't greeted them yet

These unique souls give us all inspiration

because they are strong willed

Gifted in so many areas they are so well skilled

Remember their very presence

would light up the room

When they walked away,

the aura of their personality would loom

It was not a pleasant sight

when you last saw them at the mortuary

The temperature in that room

was colder than February

Life goes on,

but it feels like it will never be the same again

That particular person was so unique among men

They had those special characteristics

that anyone could recognize

Their influence would prompt the best outcome

of a situation to materialize

When they passed over, it caused us so much anguish

For days on end, after their death we sit and languish

Our little world will seem different

without their charm

After their funeral,

life as we knew it will take on a different form

The Universal Language of Math

Math is a universal language spoken by every race

As a tool for measurement all over the world

it is commonplace

In physics and astronomy,

it is used at an advanced pace

The average person uses it to value goods

at the marketplace

Doing any form of business,

you have to communicate

the basics of math with accuracy

If you can speak math, you can speak any language

in order to obtain your foreign currency

Every person has added some knowledge

to the equations

that we use to solve a mathematical problem

You have to break the lowest denominator down

from the top to the bottom

Math speaks to everyone in every tongue

Search through them all and its influence is among

Even heavenly bodies have been created

with mathematical precision

If they go off course for a third of a second,

there would be great collision

In the cradle, our minds are programmed to count

At that tender age

we are trying to figure out the amount

Our brains are always adding and subtracting

Numbers bouncing around in our heads interacting

Everything in nature comes in pairs

and amounts to an equation

Mathematics stands at the foundation

of every culture and every nation

Look at a map of the world

and it's drawn out with an isobath

Everybody everywhere speaks

the universal language of math

<u>Constructive Criticism</u>

Constructive criticism is like the fire

that burns away impurities

Embrace the heat and melt down your insecurities

Not those negative comments, but verbal medicine

meant to cure your imperfections

This way you won't feel defeated when you are met

with rejections

We all hate to be scrutinized

But we have to listen carefully

as our faults are analyzed

Our closest loved ones

will tell us these things so candidly

And often they do it so fluently

Positive criticism is something we must withstand

It's only that negative stuff

that should fall from our ears like a grain of sand

It is not good to always be charmed
by personal praise and flattery
This isn't a good way to self-charge your battery

Criticism makes us take a look
at what needs to be changed
By correcting our flaws, so much can be gained
So it does not hurt us
to listen to other people's expertise
The solution to our problem
may be what their constructive criticism comprise

At times when someone else points out our flaws,
they seems so immense
That is why constructive criticism can penetrate
in a way that's very intense
In order to better our personalities,
this can be a powerful mechanism
Therefore, we should be receptive
to constructive criticism

Like Writer's Block

Like writer's block I wish I could erase my memory

If you know what I've been through,

there's no way you would envy me

While writing about this hurt,

I want to forget about my next line

Like writers block

I just wish I could block it out of my mind

When writing about this part of my life,

I wish I didn't remember the next verse

It's been bad, but I guess it could have been worse

So many circumstances that caused me to be a misfit

Even writer's block wouldn't let me forget

Some of these memories are like poisonous lead

That's why I try so hard to block these thoughts

from my head

Unfortunately, my brain has recorded them so clear

I have to face my past with no fear

Lost for words because my mind is an empty space

Searching for creative ways

to give my troubles a humble face

When I begin to write it down the healed wound

seems to open up again

Pouring forth fresh emotions

like a needle sticking in my skin

This is why I wish I could block it all out

Draw a blank on my mind

and forget what these events were about

Nevertheless, they bang on my mind

in a repetitive knock

Clouding my creative vision like writer's block

WORRY IS MY CONSTANT COMPANION

Why do I worry so much

It seems as if I have been cursed by anxiety's touch

Following my thoughts like a shadow

Wading through troubled waters

like a stranded paddle

Worry travels with me everywhere I go

How to deal with this dilemma I don't know

I constantly ponder on problems

that are beyond my control

Somehow my soul needs to find a peace of console

I am steadily worrying about this

and worrying about that

Turning my mind into a liability instead of an asset

It just doesn't add up

I got to burp myself from this mental hiccup

Of course, for my mind this is so unhealthy

I know this is not good mentally

Yet I can't help but worrying

The frequency of my thoughts

incoherent and flurrying

It's hard to concentrate when I am worrying

about so many things

A network of thoughts

connecting in my mind like rings

It is such a heavy burden to carry

My constant companion is worry

WOMPANION
CORRY

CAUTIOUSLY OPTIMISTIC

Looking to the future I am so optimistic,

but yet cautious

I have experienced so many failures

that it makes me nauseas

All of the opportunities that I missed is something

that I have often dreaded

That's why my motivation for progress is a seed in me

that's deeply embedded

Running through life chasing my dreams

but they are so elusive

Stuck on this road often makes my path

seem reclusive

I know that I am not alone in my desperate pursuit

Other people's dreams are constantly falling

out of the air like a parachute

Gazing through a telescope my dreams seem far off

Getting sick of my failure, my disappointment comes

up through the form of a painful cough

I go searching for medicine,

but the doctor can't give me a proper diagnosis

After studying the human mind for twenty years,

she is baffled by my psychosis

I study how some people accomplished their goals

with simplicity

Their achievements fill me with humility

I must display that same tenacity

Or else my dreams will die another casualty

Sometimes I get in over my head

and have to calm my spirit

I must ignore the doubts that whisper in my ear

when I hear it

Mapping out my future

I must account for every logistic

Traveling ahead with plans for success,

but all the while being cautiously optimistic

<u>Rhyming With Reason (Rhyming For A Reason)</u>

They ask why do I rhyme when I write my poetry

I tell them that's how I challenge myself

to break down the story

Challenging myself to convey a message

pregnant with insight

Giving birth to a new outlook

on knowledge when I write

I tend to my verses like a mother hen

Flocking the words as a shepherd with a trusty ink pen

Fleshing out the bones

my writings pulse like a heartbeat

Full of fiber for the reader

extracted from mental wheat

Insights of the intellect take on a unique meaning

to the reader of my rhymes

There is a connection with the harmony

of the universe interwoven between the lines

I write what I think and think about what I wrote

Going over the sentences again just to take note

Again, they question

why does my poetry always rhyme

Sometimes I am asked to do it different next time

If it isn't broke why should I fix it

Rhyming brings out the best of my wit

Mathematically my versus are composed

on a wavelength that is balanced rhythm

The molecules in my brain form rhymes

on every angle of the prism

Like an egg crack my verses and they give birth

to another sentence coming together in cohesion

Now I hope that you understand

that I rhyme for a reason

A PHILOSOPHER OF THE BLUES

He articulates blues like no one else can

So deep in how he explains the sadness of man

Until I was introduced to his work,

I never knew that the blues could be philosophized

But he breaks it down and show where the origin

of the sadness materialized

His thesis on the blues really makes you reflect

When it comes to his expertise on the subject

nothing is in neglect

Dealing with the root of the problem

he analyzes the soul

Therein often lies an empty spot and an unfilled hole

Most people don't know how to express their blues

Yet they feel it deeply as it colors their lives

in so many hues

Depression sets in and traps us in its throes

Sadness follows and that's where our mind goes

This artist's explanation of the blues is full of intensity
He makes sense of feelings that baffles us
with their complexity
Maybe he has a third sense of the soul
because he knows its intimacies
Connected to the blues how naturally he tunes
into its frequencies

Surprisingly he isn't just theorizing
because his philosophy consists mostly of facts
Somehow his explanation of it is so full of tact
His art is a reflection of how you feel
when you're down and out with nothing to lose
Everyone has a gift and his is being
a philosopher of the blues

I KNOW PAIN

Oh, I know pain

It clouds my sunshine and brings so much rain

I know him or should I call it her

It's this thing that keeps suffocating my air

I try to limit its space, but it keeps on making room

Sweeping across the surface like a broom

The residue from this dust keeps clouding my vision

I blow it away but still keep running into this collusion

Read the word pain and all of our stories are written

With so many letdowns

the bug of disappointment has bitten

This avalanche of sorrow seems beyond belief

Morning my own failure keeps me full of grief

It gets dark even when I am standing in the light

Why do things go wrong when I try to do what's right

Sometimes it feels like nobody understands

what I am going through

Still I stay strong because that is what my mother

taught me to do

I first felt pain when I was in my mama's womb

From conception to death I will carry it to my tomb

I blame myself for not taking the opportunities

that this world has to give

Now this life of pain is what I live

P A I N

PIECES OF US ALL

We all leave a piece of ourselves everywhere we go

Our personality circulates in the air

like a boomerang throw

A piece of me here and a piece of you there

I guess you say it's a piece of us all everywhere

Separated by artificial boarders

but our humanity makes us one whole

Uniting and finding our commonality

must be our goal

Instilling these principles in our descendants is the way

that mankind will flourish

All the spiritual blessings that God gave us

is something that we must cherish

When we come into this world,

we give ourselves a piece of it

All of us are constantly doing this

no matter where we choose to stand or sit

A piece of it goes away with the distant traveler

whether our effect is permanent or momentary

This is true no matter if our behavior

was shoddy or exemplary

Regularly we leave a piece of ourselves

wherever we may be

For the next generation we serve as an intermediary

Between our lives and theirs the history is short

By giving the best legacy that we can

is how we do our part

That's why our ancestor's legacy

is something that we must commemorate

Appreciating all that they did for us

is a reason to celebrate

Way before there was paper and pen,

they wrote their history for us on a stone wall

In this way humanity has passed on pieces of us all

THE UNTOLD STORY

Read with your heart and please don't be judgmental

as my story unfolds

Here for the first time it is being told

The copyrights to my life will never be sold

Let the humanity of our hearts warm each other

in this world that's so cold

I did not write this to paint a picture that's pretty

On the contrary the details of my life

are harsh and gritty

Yet I invite you into my world to tell you my tale

After you read this you will know it quite well

My soul is not for sale

I only release my pain so I can heal and become well

Pain and me is like a twin brother

He knows me better than any other

This pain of mine has been a great portion

of the story of my life

Even it is surprised at how I survive this strife

Growing up with addicts all around me

So confused that even I

became a victim of this tragedy

A dysfunctional family yet they wonder why

I don't always get along and function

Just walk a mile in my shoes as we cross this junction

Because I smile even though I want to cry

does that make me a lie

Why do you criticize me when I try

I get rejected even when I try to do what's right

I have been in the dark so long I am scared of the light

You say that you love the light,

but the truth will blind your eyes

So do not read this in surprise

I think you know my story so well

because it also belongs to you

Many of the events of my life are the same things

that you went through

That is why our lives tell our story together

Let's help to heal so that humanity can become better

Why are we our own worst enemy

At war with ourselves

because we fail to defeat this sentry

Let us make the world better

and stop chasing the fame and glory

Mankind this is an untold story

DANIEL'S VISION

Through divine ordinance Daniel was given a vision
At first his fear wouldn't let him see it with precision
He had asked for God's help,
but when it came, he wasn't ready
Then a hand touched him and kept him steady

In his vision saw four beasts
But each had some characteristic of a man at least
These men resembled earthly kings
Their actions were so similar to these things

These beasts were given power over the earth
On every horizon they left nothing
but destruction and hurt
Daniel's spirit was so troubled
that he did nothing but grieve
The angel Gabriel told him
God would soon give the world a relieve

He was made to understand that his vision

was the beginning of the end

God had an important message to send

The last days are here

The four beasts will bring it near

The four beasts represent four powerful kingdoms

that are corrupt

Their unholy power will suddenly come to an abrupt

For a time, it appeared that they couldn't be defeated

Then in the final onslaught of the saints,

the 4th beast retreated

God's kingdom prevailed over all

His dominion everlasting and standing tall

Heaven guided Daniel

when it was time to make a decision

It was God at the forefront of Daniel's vision

When Your Soul Is Torn In Half

Life goes on no matter what, but it gets complex

when your soul is torn in half

It's your sprung heel on top of walking through life

with a sore calf

One side of you wants to make it

but your failures try to hug your mind and cuddle

How do you pick yourself up

when you fall into this puddle

The trees of life don't even keep you company

when you are lost in this forest of solitude

In fact, in this state you want to be alone

without having anyone to intrude

Even when you keep your spirits up

your morale can be down

This even goes on with those famous people who

have a reputation that is renown

We are not talking about your soul mate because you

are the mate of your soul

If it is torn in half it is hard for you to feel whole

The soul is strong like interior structural steel

But it can be broke

if a person doesn't have a strong will

A portion of your soul is ripped with grief

due to your past mistakes

The other side is torn into a dogged determination

to succeed no matter what it takes

It's up to you to balance it out and choose

which side will prevail

You have to pick the pieces back up when you fail

The question is

how can you put it back together again

Well you must turn your loss into a win

You must nurture your soul back to health

like a cow nurtures her baby calf

This is what you must do

when your soul is torn in half

AGE SEVEN

I told her not to look back on her life in fear

But she said it was painful

when she thinks back to the seventh year

I wrote this poem for a friend

but writing it made me shed a tear

The pain from her life

makes my vision come in a blear

Seven signifies completion

For her only meant an orphan in depletion

She found no love in her home

So the streets is where she began to roam

Hell is a state of mind and so is heaven

She experienced an earthly hell

when she was just seven

The only time she felt love

was when the beautician cut her hair

It's strange that a stranger is the only one

who seemed to care

As a result of childhood scars

she is still damaged within

It's no wonder that she developed a tough skin

Trying to wash away her scars but the water is too hot

Look her in the eyes and this is what you got

I told her that it would be okay and not to worry

What she told me was that

it was a heavy burden to carry

She said that she tried to do away with this pain

when she was eleven

Now she must find a way to get rid of this pain

that she carried since age seven

THE POWER OF PATIENCE

A mystery of patience is that it is full of hidden power

Evident only to wise souls

that do not allow impatience to make them sour

Its benefit will unfold

for the discerning eye sees beyond the physical

A person has to go within and tune into the mystical

At times it is difficult to be patient,

but it is for our own benefit

In fact, instead of shying away,

we should fully embrace it

Patience teaches us how to endure

In addition, how to do without

when we think we need more

The value of patience is found in its aftermath

Allowing those who understand

to find jewels along the path

Walk the line of patience and cross into wisdom's lane

Appreciate the blessings of the struggle while knowing

that your waiting is not in vain

Have patience while seeing the picture that is bigger

The now moments shape the future

is what you should figure

Be patient from understanding

and not just for patience sake

The things that you go through

define the ultimate person you will make

Slow down and you will experience life from all sides

Seeing beautiful colors that a fast-paced life often hides

Impatience disturbs peace and the joy of life

it tends to devour

Wait with steadfastness and you will experience

patience power

UNTAMED EMOTION

We voice our emotions in words or actions

Depending on what gives us satisfaction

Still emotions have their own lyric

Guided by a person's spirit

Emotion has a voice all its own

Never half hearted because it is full blown

Floating on a bubble about to burst

Landing haphazardly about to crash face first

Good or bad takes on its own form

Depending on the source,

emotions can cause great harm

That is why emotions should be controlled

Otherwise, chaos can take a hold

Untamed emotions can destroy relationships

like a tornado

Blowing down foundations that took years to grow

It is best that we try to keep emotions tamed

Not bottled up but properly framed

Emotions also have their own personality

No matter the source, they all share commonality

If not checked, they can cause a lot of commotion

This is what happens

when we are controlled by emotion

EMOTIONS

SLEEPLESS NIGHTS

I am just laying here, but I cannot go to sleep
Tossing and turning then balling up into a heap
Under the blanket with my eyes closed,
but my thoughts are so open
Just drift off into a deep hole is what I am hoping

No matter what I do my thoughts just will not rest
Pondering about all these things
is really starting to be a pest
My body is tired, but my brain is so energized
Sleepy eyes yet I'm so restless
sleep cannot be recognized

Nights like this feel like they will never end
Wanting to go to sleep
only if my mind had some rest to lend
It is very active when it should be shutting down

Flooding my brain and making my intuition drown

Trying to pass time but time passed,

and the night is still early

A full moon shining through bright and pearly

I lay my head down

while my thoughts are up there with the stars

Thinking about the life that exist on the planet Mars

The end of the night seems to fade into the dark

This is the point where the road breaks off into a fork

My restless mind keeps on seeing all of these sights

Tomorrow takes forever to come when I am having

one of those sleepless nights

A WRITERS VOW

Before a word is written,

a writer makes a vow to their soul

A promise to get the truth across is their main goal

They want to tell the story in a way that the character

possessed them to see, feel, and say

This becomes an obsession of theirs

each and every day

The marriage of the words to the paper

comes without a ceremony

There is a no guarantee that the relationship

will be lived in holy matrimony

Nevertheless, it's still for better or worse through

sickness and in health till death do them part

The art and the artist have an intimate bond from

the mind, soul, and heart.

It is a silent vow,

but it screams inside of the writer's being

Inspiring them with mental visions

that only they are seeing

Them with their ink pen, they embark on a mission

where sometimes they do not know

where they are going

Yet they continue along that path as long as the truth

is the vehicle that keeps their sentences flowing

When a sincere writer tells a story,

it bothers them to deviate from the truth even slightly

Remembering their vow

is not something they take lightly

Within themselves that is a promise that they hold

themselves accountable for

Even when recording the history of ancestors,

they search the facts

not settling for tradition and family lore

The script writes itself out

in the depth of the writer's mind

Searching out ways to tell a truth

that it promised to find

To uncover hidden details the characters use telepathy

to tell the author how

In the end, the final product is a true testament

of upholding a writer's vow

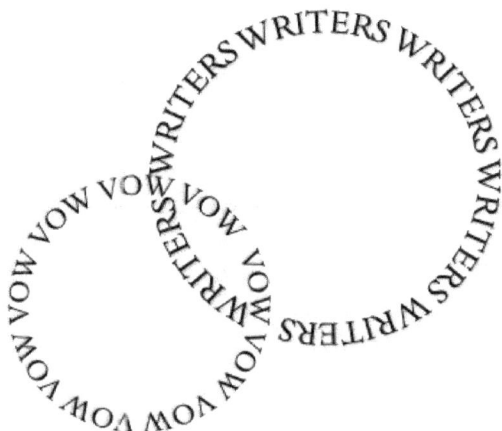

WHEN YOU JUST WANT TO LIVE AGAIN

Life at its worst makes you feel like you are just

going through the motions

Dead on the inside, but from the outside nobody

can tell that you're experiencing these notions

Carrying on as usual though usually

you don't feel like this

Thinking about the good times

doesn't even lift your spirits when you reminisce

Physically you exist but you don't feel alive

The experience of true life

is the goal for which you strive

I know that other people take it for granted

Horizontally they move through life

in an angle that is slanted

On the inside, you feel dead, but your heart

is still beating and your mind is thinking

The inner you is falling further into an abyss

while sinking

You just want to see the light

and get your life back to where it used to be

Then maybe it will not be so difficult

to attain prosperity

Nobody wants to be dead or alive dead

We would rather be full of like instead

Living can take you all the way under

Moving through life

you will sometimes trip and blunder

During these times you must do everything

that you can to get your life back

In this quest there is no room

to procrastinate and slack

As each struggle ends, another one is sure to begin

That's just life so we have to live it to the fullest when

you just want to live again

ENDLESS DAYS

Days like this are the ones that feel like

they will never end

Time becomes the enemy

because there is too much of it to spend

Everything seems to be going wrong,

yet the times will not change

Heavy is the burden that's starving my joy

like a hunger pang

We find things to do but the days still just

slowly drag on by

A slow minute can feel like an hour

and that's time alibi

It was not where we thought it should be,

so we charged it with missing

We could not prove it because the hands of the clock

didn't need a fixing

I am counting too far ahead,

and the time just will not come fast enough

The burden of these endless days can be rough

Time doesn't stand still even though

right now, it is going slow

Waiting on a better future

but it doesn't seem to want to show

It's hard waiting on time

when time will not wait on you

Left with no choices because being patient

is all you can do

Still that doesn't end the matter

Looking at an empty dish with time as the platter

Eat up the time and don't let the slowness of it

eat you up inside

In its boundaries we will always reside

When things are moving slowly,

we have to pass time in creative ways

Life in itself is full of endless days

I FELL IN LOVE WITH HER INTERVIEW

Just reading her responses to a reporter's questions

had me smitten

Overlapping my own fancy was the introspective

words that the journalist had written

Everything that she said

just took my mind into another sphere

Her intellect sparkens articulating her vision so clear

Deeply I gained insight into her view

from the inner side

Inside the view was a mirror reflecting

the ambition we all hide

She handles her business

with so much precision and grace

All the while humanity and deepness as the features

reflect from her face

How did she wisen and mature to know

all that she does know

A boss lady she runs the show

Modern yet she has the style of women

from antiquity way back

Working hard at what she does

not even giving herself any slack

From my awe you would think I am talking about

a superstar or famous entertainer

To accomplish all that she did makes you assume

she had the help of a coach or renown trainer

On the contrary she is self-taught

and only a literary editor

A woman of our times who built an empire

while crushing her competitors

Of course, I have loved the interviews of famous

women singers, dancers, entrepreneurs,

and the artistic elite

Yet I didn't fall in love with their mind the way that

this editor captured my delight

Her body of work shows that to her vision

she is forever true

Across different cultures her mind grabbed me

and I fell in love with her interview

Time Waits For No Man

My mama told me that time waits for no man
This is a fact that we must truly understand
We have to continue to complete our life plans
In this world we only have a short lifespan

Time is precious
That's why we have to reassess
Although there is a lot of things we have to get done
Too much rest is not always good
because time is on the run

When humans get very tired and stop
Time forever runs on the clock
We can't race against time because we will not win
Sometimes time can be our enemy
and then at other times it can be our friend

Most of us here on this planet have time on our side

There's a lot we can accomplish as long as we are alive

Some people say that we are in a race against time

Life goes on going forward not in rewind

Time is a resource that must be used in reason

It plays all four seasons

When it comes down to time,

sometimes we are forced to take a chance

Time waits for no man and it may leave us

in an unworthy circumstance

It Isn't Easy To Talk About Your Pain

It most definitely is not always easy
to talk about your pain
When you do you tend to feel the cold rain
Do you relive the pain when you speak about it
Even in silence your soul shouts it

You must try to heal these wounds
Scars of this type often get buried in our inner tomb

Can you stand the pain
Is it too heavy a burden on your brain
Internal pain is not easy to heal
Deep down it is something that you feel

Some pain is straight with no chase
Right there looking at you in the face
It is something that you hate to bear

Yeah pain is not easy to share

Sometimes our pain is internal

It hits the light and cannot be escaped

through a tunnel

Throughout it all you must be strong and stay sane

Try to express it even though it is not easy

to talk about your pain

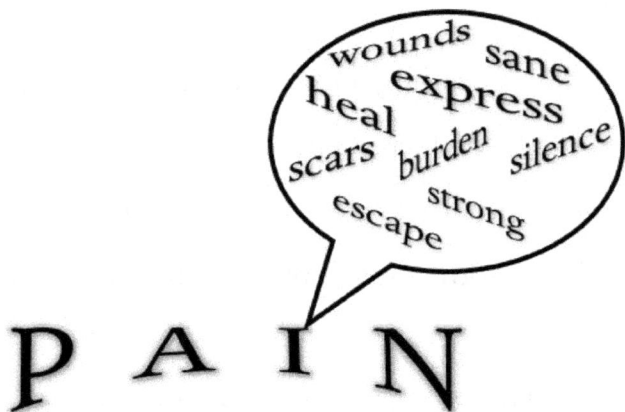

wounds sane
heal express
scars burden silence
escape strong

P A I N

Two Wrongs Don't Make A Right

When someone does something wrong to us,

we gear up to fight

A conscience thought should remind us that

two wrongs don't make a right

Then comes another though with revenge

as its insight

Our lesser selves then proceed

to avenge our injury with all our might

Avenging our injury is not always the best way

Behind unjustified violence is a consequence to pay

How can two wrongs committed by two people

make a situation the right one

When you both take a fall, nobody won

I know that seeking get back

is a notion to fulfill when someone does you wrong

However, I hope you give a lot of thought

before the first blow is thrown

Two wrongs doesn't make anything right

Some see it as a way of surviving life

Seeking revenge is at the heart

of so many of my mistakes

At times I have lost all that was at stake

Hurting someone out of revenge

is not going to make the hurt go away

If the tables turn, what will you have to say

Try to put it out of your mind

So it will not be the first in your sight

Weigh whether or not two wrongs make a right

Mama I Wish You Would Understand

Mama I wish you would understand

I have to live my own life

and not the one that you planned

I know that you have good intentions

Still I cannot live by your strict set of restrictions

Now that I am old enough to tell you

I have to let you know

I am grown now, and you cannot run my life

like a well-orchestrated show

I will never stop listening to your advice

It's just that now it is time for me to live my own life

I will always be your child

Just because I'm no longer living under your roof,

I will not start acting wild

I'll never forget the many lessons that you taught me

Nobody can ever replace these memories

I know that in your eyes I will always be your baby
But when you treat me like a little child
it drives me crazy
You will forever be number one in my world
The values that you instilled in me
will always be my first referral

I know sometimes you feel helpless
when I do different from what you say
However, you should know that the golden rules that
you set for me I will always obey
Sometimes you just have to let me learn
the hard way on my own
That is a consequence I must learn
from thinking that I am so grown

Bad Breaks and Setbacks

In life we have to face the facts

There will always be bad breaks and setbacks

These are obstacles that get in the way of our plans

They may leave us in an undesirable circumstance

A bad break is a break

that we usually do not ask to get

Yet it is something that we have to deal with

Sometimes you may have a project to complete

Then you'll see one mistake that you cannot delete

Bad breaks can come in the form

of a disappointment or a let-down

This does not mean that a failure has to be bound

We just have to keep trying harder

Finding ways to make things better tomorrow

You may wish to achieve a certain goal but face an

immediate setback

To give up will be the wrong way to act

Things may not progress as quick as we like

Anything that we wish to accomplish in life

requires a fight

Bad breaks and setbacks are a part of life

So, we have to overcome such strife

After a bad break we must continue to strive

After enduring these setbacks,

we must keep hope alive

If You Could Change The Hands Of Time

If you could rewind your life

would you try to live it different again

Where would you stop and where would you begin

You can never change the past,

but you will be able to learn from your mistake

You will have similar options

but different paths to take

How would you do things differently

Would the choices that you make today be healthy

If you were to think off of your emotions

would you fall into the same traps

Will the format of your current life precede the

outline of your previous life maps

If you could change, your life would probably

be as good as you want it to be

In the end you must still live out the results

of your destiny

The outcomes of our lives

are said to already be destined

It has also been noted

that the prophecy of this should be questioned

Supposing that you could rewind back

the hands of time

You would be discouraged by a lot of things

you will find

Events of your past may not be as vividly

as you picture them to be

So many new experiences has invaded and influenced

your mental capacity

Would you be willing to relive the most

painful moments of darkness when there was no light

Do you think you are really strong enough

to repeat this fight

Reflect on how life kindles the electricity in your mind

Then make the decision of whether or not you would

change the hands of time

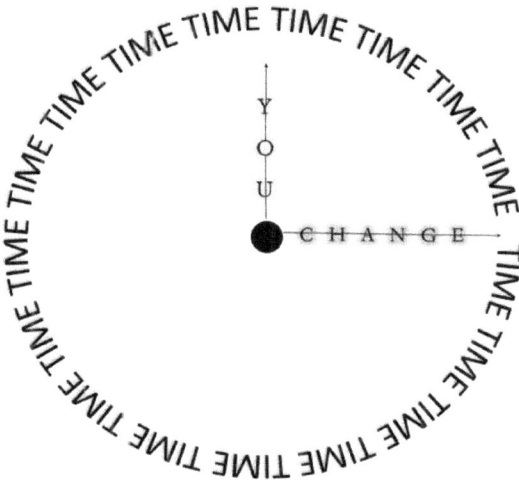

It Isn't Always Easy To Do What We Say

It isn't always easy to do what we say

Things will become more harder for us this way

Sometimes we make plans that we don't stick to

We will keep putting them to the side

because of other things we had to do

At times we have good intentions

to do the things we say

But when it comes down to it things don't be that way

Life changes all the time

Just as often as we change our minds

We say things that we really believe

we are going to do

But once that time comes, we have to pay other dues

Sometimes when we say things,

we have the best of intention

Yet there's other things we've committed to

that our mind failed to mention

The average person is not organized and disciplined

enough to do everything that they say

Life can always put you in a different situation

and another place

We never know where we may be

tomorrow or next week

Life itself is forever growing to another peak

Everything that we commit

to is not always within our range

One thing that is certain about life is change

In this uncertain life, we never know

what might happen the next day

That is why it is hard to abide by all the things that we

say

TRIALS, TRIBES, AND TRIBULATIONS

We all face trials, tribes, and tribulations

As the result of all unpredictable situations

Whatever it is in life that you may do

There will be certain trials, tribes,

and tribulations that await you

Facing trials, tribes, and tribulations

is sometimes for the best

Living the life of a human

will always put you to the test

It's a process that every man, woman,

and child must go through

When we receive pay we must turn over our due

Trials, trials and what they stand for

Some people never want to face them any more

Trials, trials, trials and the inspiration

that they may give

We face thousands of them
even though we only have one life to live

Tribes, tribes, tribes
and the numerous numbers that they come in
All odds against you and it seems you'll never win
Tribes, tribes, tribes
and the obstacles that they leave along the way
We may face several tribes everyday

Tribulations, tribulations, tribulations
and the traps that they met
The good things you try to remember and bad ones
you would rather forget
Tribulations, tribulations, tribulations
and the stress they keep at surface
We must not let this take us under
as we strive to overcome this

Going through trials, tribes, and tribulations

only make us stronger

I do not look at trials, tribes, and tribulations

as a problem any longer

So, oh trials, tribes, and tribulations show me the way

Give me strength after I overcome you today

```
        T
        R
T R I B U L A T I O N S
        A         R
        L         I
        S         B
                  E
                  S
```

WE ALL PAY THE PRICE FOR SOMEONE ELSE

We all pay the price for someone else

Whether we do it on accident or on purpose

Our downfall will be the next person's rise

A setback in our position may be their prize

Someone paid the price for us

to get where we have got

Even though we may not admit this a lot

Without the generations before us

where would we be today

The world probably wouldn't have

its technology sway

Thus the generation before us

paid the price for our generation

When they reached milestones for us

they didn't expect compensation

We are all an example for someone else to learn from

The mistakes that we have made will benefit

the next generation to come

In some way we all pay the price for the next person

The success of our audition saved them time

that would have been spent rehearsing

We must continue to help others

and not only think of our self

In life we all pay the price for someone else.

G
E
N
E
R
A
T
I
O
N
S

Sometimes It's Hard To Survive

It has been said that to survive
is to find meaning in suffering
Without struggle you will gain nothing
Sometimes it's hard trying to get by
Especially after your problems seem to multiply

For one to live is for one to suffer
Life mandates that you withstand
all that you can muster

Survival calls on one to have a strong will
At times a person will have to keep working
no matter how tired they feel
So, our struggles may be harder
When things get tough,
we must keep our head above the water

Throughout all of your hard times

you must not lose hope

When you get stressed out

you must find some way to cope

So, if you fail at least you know that you tried

When you fall pick yourself back up

because it is hard to survive

```
                    L

                    I

                    V

S  U  R  V  I  V  E

U

F

F

E

R
```

SURVIVING THE PUNCHES THAT LIFE THROWS AT ME

It's an everyday struggle to survive

the punches that life throws at me

I must keep my head up and face reality

Day after day this is how things must be

Keeping my eyes wide open so I can see

How many blows and struggles

does one have to endure

People feel insecure about themselves

just because they are poor

I am so young but have been through so much

I've tried the easy way but when it comes to life

there is no shortcut

I haven't walked on the face of this earth 20 years

Yet already I have cried over 2 million tears

Without struggle one can never be perfected

My old ways must die off so I can become resurrected

I will continue to survive this heartache and pain

Before the sun shines it has to rain

After going through all of my troubles

I still have my sanity

I understand the fact that life is not all fine and dainty

There is consequences to everything that you do

In the end, you have to survive

the punches that life throws at you

Things Aren't Always what They Seem To Be

Things are not always what they seem to be
You may be intrigued by an illusion
and think that it's reality
I know you have heard the saying that things
are not always what they seem
Do you really know what this means

When you are looking at something
you must see the big picture to take it all in
Afterwards you can see what is really within
Before you buy off into something
you must study it inside-out
This is the only way you will truly know
what it is about

We all have purchased something

that turned out to be not as good as we thought

But we couldn't take it back after it was bought

After incidents like this,

some of us still haven't learned

So, we keep taking chances that leave us burned

Outside appearances can carry a false illusion

Therefore, do not become bewildered

by the confusion

Look past the smokescreen

and do not sell yourself a dream

You must come to realize

that things aren't always what they seem

SEEKING TO ORGANIZE MY UNPROFESSIONAL TALENT

I have to find a way to organize

my unprofessional talent

Every obstacle that I face is a challenge

I have talent that I must begin to use

Running the streets all my life is not what I choose

I must not let the various talents that I possess

go to waste

So, I indeed must seek to organize it with haste

I must conquer patience and learn to wait

Manifest my intellect up to date

I have come to this conclusion at last

In the last 8 years hustling in these streets

was my only use of math

I have to change my negative ways of getting by in life

Striving to make a living by doing what's right

Higher education has always been of interest to me

I want to become the best businessman

that I can possibly be

I will start today to organize my unprofessional talent

I refuse to let it be of the extravagant

So, before I let my mind become a useless package

I will do everything in my power

to organize my unprofessional talent

Make The Best Of The Worst

Sometimes we have to make the best of the worst

While coming to understand that the world

is not under some curse

Before you experience the good

you have to go through the bad first

You can improve your conditions

as long as you are on the earth

My mama told me that son sometimes life is not fair

But there is good people that always care

Grandma used to say that it got to get worse

before it can get better

I always wonder why she put this in my get-well letter

I never understood what you said

until I began to mature and grow

I saw that good times go fast, while bad times go slow

Granddad told me I got it way easier

than he did at my age

I didn't believe him till he opened his photo album

and turned the first page

He told me to count my blessing

But he knew I hadn't learned my lesson

I still sometimes complain about how things are today

Not realizing it was harder yesterday

No matter how bad it was

mama said to make the best of it

Some people have it worse than this

I asked my mama

how can I make the best of the worst

When they buried my little brother in the dirt

Someone said no longer will that person hurt

He left this earth by making the best of the worst

THE THINGS THAT WE DO FOR MONEY

There's no limit to the things that some of us
will do for money
We will commit so much evil that it isn't even funny
Some of us will do inhumane things to obtain wealth
Even if it may be at the cost of someone else's health

Some of us do things to get money
for chemical reasons
Because we have a distorted need
to support our drug habits through all seasons
For a lot of our mistakes, money was the cause
So, before we do things
we need to think and take a pause

Although we need money to purchase

the essentials in life

To fulfill our wants,

money takes us through un-warranting strife

Money allows some people of the world to be content

while the majority is left hurt

In the end money seldom extends to its worth

Is it in God or in money that we trust

The truth about this is worth a lot of fuss

Some of us put money before everything

We use stimulants to erase our conscience clean

We all sometimes fall victim to that dollar bill

In the end we'll wonder about all the trouble and zeal

Even if we don't have wealth the sky will still be sunny

So we need to put a limit to

the things that we do for money

Get In Touch With Your Inner Self

We must get in touch with our inner selves

This way we will not be affected

by the opinions of someone else

Have you ever been told

that you have all the answers to everything

Have you ever tried

to put the pieces together of your dreams

We must learn to nurture our soul

Then we can get our lives under control

Our inner selves consists partially of our faith

If we have determination, we can climb over any gate

When a person truly knows themselves,

they understand

that what others think of them is irrelevant

Problems of today have to be conquered like the ones

of yesterday that came and went

After getting in tune with your inner self

you will see your major fault

You will work harder to correct things

knowing that hope is never lost

Within yourself you will find the strength

to fight any battle

Acquiring leadership skills that will allow you

to shepherd a stubborn herd of cattle

Have you ever been told

that all you have to do is put your mind to it

The truth to this is that all you have to do

is keep trying and don't quit

We all must strive to know

what's inside of our own inner being

Then we can learn to overcome all of the out things

It is what is inside of us that holds us back

Once we get in touch with our inner self,

we can get on the right track

I

N

N

S E L F

R

<u>We Need To Listen To Our Conscience</u>

Many of us ignore our conscience too much
It seeks to remind us to stay spiritually in touch

Our conscience is our guide
By the rules that God set it will abide
In its natural state our conscience
is obedient to God's law
It reminds us that living unrighteously is a flaw

People's conscience brings about their guilt
It is their inner built in a holy quilt
It is healthy for our souls
Although sometimes it seems
to put more weight on our loads

Our conscience is with us everywhere we go

It tells us when to move fast or when to move slow

Our conscience tells us not to live our life fast

When we do, we usually don't last

If you haven't repented to God,

your conscience isn't clear

None of our lives are pure

We all need to seek God's repentance

Just as we need to listen to our conscience

TOMORROW BRINGS BETTER DAYS

I was having a difficult day, and someone said

tomorrow brings better days

It was hard for me to see

when it was all turning out in the wrong ways

Everyday it only seemed to get worse

My pain needed more than a common nurse

Again, others said hold on

because times will get better

The forecast for tomorrow promises sunny weather

We live in a world where negativity seems to rule

But the positive is what we must choose

Tomorrow will bring you closer to better days

Showing you the way of exit out of this dark maze

Overcome the madness

You know you deserve some happiness

A form of heaven as well as hell can be experienced

right here on this earth

What are your deeds worth

Keep doing the good

You will reap what you should

I am tired of being down because of my poverty

Tomorrow God's promised land will be the place

I hope to live on the property

Let us do away with our negative ways

Look to the future because surely tomorrow

will bring better days

IMAGE IS EVERYTHING

In this unconscious world, image is everything
People are living off of fantasies and unrealistic dreams
Status and clout depend on wealth
People are doing things for attention
that is very bad for their health

Everyone is concerned with achieving rank
Clothing themselves with material things
and distorting their thinking tank
Too many people are concerned
with what someone else is receiving
It is only themselves that they are deceiving

So many of us seek fortune and fame
Wishing for stardom to be associated with our name
So many people seek an image that is not theirs
Taking on the persona of someone else's affairs

We cannot be anyone but ourselves

Leaving the personality of other people

on their shelves

This is the way that it should be

Let's accept our humble reality

A person is human just like you

no matter what they have

Yours is yours and theirs is for them to grab

I once wrote that everything is not what it seems

Yet in this fickle world image is everything

The Majority Of Us Need To Realize How Blessed We Are

The majority of us need to realize how blessed we are

Many of our families are fortunate enough

to have a house and car

We need to start appreciating the little things

Understanding what the value of being alive means

There are some people who can't read, see, or write

They'll give anything in the world

just to be able to see the sunlight

Some people can't even speak or talk

Others are handicap and cannot walk

Some of us have things that others will die for

Many of us obtained freedom

through a revolutionary war

Some people do not even have money

to afford shoes to wear on their feet

While others possess more than enough to eat

Many of us are blessed with various skills

Fortunate enough to have our talents to pay our bills

Others struggle to find a roof

to put over their family's head

While others lay down every night in a luxurious bed

We have to be content with our unique abilities

Gifts that we have, become sacred responsibilities

Some are afflicted by internal and external pain

from a scar

A prime example for the rest of us

to realize how blessed we are

The Birth Of The Book

As I read the introduction,

I wonder how does an author give birth to a book

That thought alone made me scan the last chapter

for a second look

From the beginning to the end, the entire story

seemed to be a mystery even to the writer themselves

Throughout the embryo of the book, they wondered

if it would have a healthy delivery at the bookshelves

How do you know what's in the womb of your mind

even when you cannot see it

Pregnant with a rich idea that is conceived

through a piece of lit

Giving birth to a book sometimes takes years

Challenging you to push harder as your creative

intuition shifts into higher gears

In the first trimester you are only concerned with

bringing this idea into this world

Prenatal you nurture it like a publisher with urgent

dispatchers to herald

When the first seeds of the book

have just been planted

You must plow the characters of their true feelings,

and not the rubbish of people

who just rove and ranted

Entering the second trimester

the book takes on a life of its own

Kicking and growing into a new life far beyond what

your imagination had first known

Attached to the umbilical cord of your mind

like flesh and blood

Before you go into the delivery phase, you must edit

so the plots and subplots don't overflood

From conception to development,

book birthing is full of leaps

of progress as well as hidden pitfalls

Like having children, it is intensive and exhausting,

as well as loaded with overhauls

As in parenthood even after the birth,

the work continues with more

than you thought it would've took

Postpartum marketing selling with extra promotion to

give a happy childhood after the birth of the book

PUSHING THE ENVELOPE

Inside the envelope rests the blueprint, check, or

document we need to launch our career

Outside we handle its contents carefully

and always keep it near

In our anticipation,

we may even already have the postage affixed

This is where our motivation, determination,

and desire is mixed

The envelope can be symbolic

of many things in our lives

If circumstances threaten it to go under,

we must take many dives

Traveling in the oceans of life,

we are just a few miles from our dearest dream

Like a kayaker,

we must push the paddle harder going upstream

At times we keep the envelope,

you will meet obstacles and resistance

Just keep pushing and soon you get aid and assistance

No matter how hard it seems at first

you must keep on pushing

Sometimes going against the grain

is where the vein of oil will go out gushing

Keep track of your envelope

as you deliver it to its destination

Monitor its contents and let what's inside

be your demonstration

Then it will deliver on its promise and potential

and fulfill your greatest hope

Therefore, with all your might, you must continue

to push the envelope

A Wakened Intellect

When I was 18 years old

my intellect experienced a rebirth

when I heard the written word recited and spoken

There and then my intellect was again re-awoken

Before that it had been kind of dormant and idle

Only flirting with knowledge with no working title

Through books I felt the texture of language

that was emotional and raw

Also studying heavy scientific papers

made my cold brain thaw

Warming me up to the undiscovered world

of intelligence

A new freedom for my knowledge

became my providence

Now my mind wants to know a little something about

every scientific discipline

From astronomy to zoology

back to archaeology, the study of men

I have developed an unquenchable appetite

for learning

Therefore, my intellect is always churning

Never will I allow my intellect to go back to sleep

Nor will it be shallow because

I'll always keep my mind deep

Investigating life and all its wonders

Breaking down scientific theories

separating proven facts from the flounders

In my constant quest for knowledge

I give my all to that endeavor

Hoping to acquire a little wisdom from mentors

that I consider to be clever

Now 18 years later

I reflect on all of my previous studies in retrospect

I was blessed the day I was gifted with

an awakened intellect

WHEN LIFE WEIGHS YOU DOWN

Sometimes the burden gets heavy to carry

and life seems unfair

Nevertheless, don't think about giving up

don't you dare

The burdens of life will weigh us down

time and time again

These are the times that we must use

our reserved strength every now and then

I know that being strong can be easier said than done

Without doing so though,

will cause the problems of life to steal away our fun

The sadness of being down is harder to do

than keeping the joy of being upbeat

Another one of life's contradictions that we will meet

Happiness is that feeling

that keeps alluding us from its capture

It scantily allows us to immerse in its rapture

The problem is that we just keep looking for it

in the wrong places

Instead of looking for it within ourselves, we

erroneously look for it in things and faces

Get from up under the weight of life

and live at the summit

Don't keep letting it bring you down but learn from it

It is often said that we must embrace life

and the many opportunities it has to offer

Aiming for success in our destiny with the precision

of hitting a hole in one like a golfer

Yes, I know that life can make you tense

Still you must not forget that happiness of good times

is a thought away if you reminisce

Better times will indeed come around

Remember this when life weighs you down

WHEN FREEDOM SEEMS SO FAR AWAY

Have you ever been trapped,

and freedom seemed so far out of your reach

Grab for it as you may

but its boundaries are difficult to breach

As human beings we seek to be free

from many a thing

Locked away from our dreams

and the bells of freedom don't ring

On the run but yet we are so often captured

Just the thought of true freedom

leaves our minds enraptured

The possibilities to be free from personal prisons

steadily lurking on the surface

We long to escape from this harsh reality

so we can experience bliss

Fervently we chase after freedom,

but it continues to allude

Disrupting and dismantling our optimistic mood

Yet we will always continue this lifelong pursuit

Freedom is that God given right embedded

deep down in our root

Just to be free is what we long for

Not to remain in captivity any more

Ironically, it's us that sometimes is our own

greatest oppressor

Freeing ourselves merely consist of a great effort

to stop settling for lessor

So, ask yourself what must you do

to free yourself from captivity

Give your best effort

when you engage in this strenuous activity

It is an uphill battle, but it will be worth it when you

reach the top at the end of the day

Until we conquer our personal problems,

freedom will remain so far away

FREEDOM

TIMELESS CLASSICS

There is something about a timeless classic

that gives you goose bumps

Hearing one or reading one

makes your heart throb with triple pumps

It causes us to wonder how could one artist talent be

so great

that masterpiece was created in one take

The surprising thing about most classics

is that they were done in only one session

A burst of creative genius displayed teaching countless

generations a timeless lesson

Mentally study the work and watch how it works

all through your body and mind

With so many jewels in one place making it a rare find

Classic because it's one of a kind

Repeat play stop go back and rewind

Timeless because it stands through the test of time

Great through the ages,

a diamond in the dirt amongst the grime

A classic is rare because its uniqueness stands out

from anything that was contemporary

Somehow a miracle within itself

how it holds its own testimony

Try as they may, but no one does with the material

what the originator did

There lies in that body of work evident traces

of where their genius hid

Original and not to be duplicated

Classic in the way that it was created

Be always prepared to become overcome with awe

when you are entertained by these theatrics

Works of art like these have been crafted onto history

as timeless classics

Full On Life

Right now, you can't even buy this joy

that I am feeling

Happiness like this is the natural way of healing

Yes, it's true that life is for the living

The gift of life is the ultimate act of giving

Just look at the world

with all the wonderful things before you

This is a simple remedy

for when you are feeling down and blue

Mind the diamonds that are in you and watch

how your continence sparkens

Allow your inner light to shine

when the world around you darkens

Periodically life can get us down a bit

During these times, just be grateful

for all of the blessings that you get

There are so many

that you will not be able to keep count

Look a little closer and realize how many divine gifts

overrun at your fount

No matter what you are going through,

you must continue to live

Experience all of the blessings that life has to give

Appreciate life for what it is worth

Then you will be filled with happiness and mirth

Keep flying on the high of life and fly higher

when it brings you down

Solitude is good, but every blue moon to have fun

you should spend a night out on the town

Life in itself can be a wild ride,

so grab the horns of the bull

Eat your fill because the miracle of life

offers enough substance to keep us full

My Ode To Poetry

I love what poetry can do

The credit for its contribution to language

is long overdo

What poetry does with language

can't be done in any other form

To that timeless art I write this poem

Poetry is that oldy but goody

Memories of timeless stanzas in your head

can't be covered with a hoodie

They just keep playing themselves in your brain

over and over again

Poetic versus taking your mind for a spin

Some poetry is heavy,

but its weight can't be measured

Its words just drop jewels on your mind

that must be forever treasured

Other poems are light with metaphors

that are easy to carry

Words full of delight that leave you happy and merry

Poetry dedicates itself to every occasion

Capturing history in words of emotional persuasion

See how a poem just consumes your entire soul

Words in spirit connecting the parts to the whole

A mystery but yet its secrets are open to everyone

Unlocking our deepest emotions

shining the light of its sun

Helping us to heal from our hurts

when we write it to find meaning in our own story

As an admirer to this unique artform

I dedicate his ode to poetry

A Work In Progress

Life within itself is a constant work in progress

Everyone is striving for some level of success

Once you accomplish one goal,

you must move on to the next one

However, which we look at it,

our work never seems to be done

When an invention is complete

someone comes later and adds something on

It appears that our scientific conclusions

are never foregone

Scientists still in the lab

tinkering with theories from centuries ago

The progress of man is advanced in some areas,

while in others it is slow

Everything in nature progresses in degrees

No one ever said that this life would be lived with ease

That's why we constantly have work to do

Sometimes it just comes up impromptu

I'm always working, and I work hard

Trying to save myself because I'm my own lifeguard

Swimming through life without a boat

Inhale exhale I must stay afloat

We are all a work in progress,

so I guess our work never ends

Attempting to get to a comfortable place,

but getting caught up in these whirlwinds

I just say a prayer and ask God to bless

Without Him none of our work will progress

POVERTY STRICKEN CHILDREN

Born into this world in poverty
due to forces beyond their control
Wealth that should have went to them
is something some corrupt government stole
Food is scarce so there is hardly ever enough
to fill their appetite
At mealtime, instead of getting a spoonful
they can only take a bite

Agriculture is advanced,
yet the farmers aren't tilling the seeds to cultivate
So nutritional vegetables and fruit are not being
produced at a sufficient rate
As a result, we have all of these hungry kids
It makes you wonder why are so many contractors
putting in outrageous bids

Look at these innocent children

being robbed of their childhood

They grew up very fast and are often misunderstood

Due to no fault of their own,

why do they have to suffer like this for

With no money, they still have to pay the price

of being poor

Poverty has stricken these children

in a wide-spread outbreak

Threatening to kill them off

because of humanity's mistake

Every child should be fed and clothed

Guaranteed an education and every government

that doesn't do this should be loathed

What's wrong with mankind

when we don't provide for our greatest asset

These children's lives and well-being

are something that we must protect

Shame on us because we put so much value

on our own personal property

The world can only blame itself

for having so many children being stuck in poverty

The Mystery Of Language

Language is near the top

of mankind's most profoundest mystery

Constantly evolving itself over time

throughout history

Telling the story of the universe

changing as the universe does

Warning us of the future

while explaining the past of what was

Language is spoken and it is written

Coming in thousands of scripts and tongues,

it can leave your mind bitten

Each culture across the globe has their own dialect

Semantics used as architecture to build up intellect

Old languages die out and new ones are born

Really just reinventing themselves in another form

When it was written, writing must be a demonstration

Spoken into existence from a work of art

crafted after calculation

In its countless forms, language can be even unspoken

Even failing to communicate its message

like a promise that is broken

Different languages explaining the same things

in different ways

Lost in translation, condemnation

somehow turns into praise

How each race, nation, and tribe

birthed their own language remains a wonder

Question as to where to place each syllable

and how many alphabets by the number

I know this language,

but my knowledge of foreign languages

is infant as a newborn baby

I want to at least learn one or two of them

in my lifetime before I die maybe

In this land I have educated myself

all the way to college

With foreign language, I am still in preschool

with my little knowledge

That's why I have the greatest respect for

professors of language's history

They teach the origins of languages trying to help us

to unravel the mystery

A TITLE WITHOUT A NAME

A title is supposed to name something

so how could it not have a name

If it doesn't properly identify the object,

then it's all the same

A sign can be a title or even a symbol

As long as the content and the product resemble

There are titles of different ranks and positions

Also, those of the songs of various musicians

It seems that there is a title for just about everything

Up from the leaders of our countries

down to the songs that we sing

Naming the title identifies what you are looking for

Without the proper guide, you will get lost on the

tour

Without a guide, you will get lost on the tour

Make sure that the title and the description matches

For you then will come the right dispatches

Other titles seem misleading of their alphabet

Upon them was bestowed a destination

for which hasn't been met

You call it this, they call it that

Where was that title named at

In every era title can sometimes be confusing

Yet another form of language abusing

Title it what you may, but keep it original to its fame

Behold a title without a name

When You Are Inspired, You Are An Inspiration

When you are inspired,

you take your efforts to the next level

Digging yourself out of holes

you become an expert at using a shovel

Soon other people begin to take notice

of your movements

This inspires them to make

their own self-improvements

Extra energy circulates through your system

when you are inspired

A deep passion for your goals seldom gets you tired

People in positions above you don't understand your

moves, so you move without their permission

Everybody around you

can see that you are on a mission

The inspiration from your presence

begins to spread in the air

Others pick it up because it's hard to resist

and not share

Every time someone inspires me, I am deeply affected

Their accomplishments remind me

of the efforts I have neglected

Most people serve as an inspiration to others

without them even knowing

This is because it's not their words

but their actions that are showing

Whatever they say they set out and do

In turn this serves as inspiration to you

It's not only their lecture

but their success record that truly inspired us

So, when they are speaking, we excuse their language

when they let out the occasional cuss

The actions that you take as a result of their positive

energy is a mechanism for motivation

When you are inspired you are an inspiration

```
                            M
    I N S P I R A T I O N
    N                   T
    S                   I
    P A S S I O N       V
    I       U           A
    R       C           T
    E       C           I
            E           O
            S           N
            S
```

WHAT ARE WE THINKING

Who told humans that when they eat an apple
that they shouldn't eat the core
Nobody ponders on questions like these anymore
People only start planning
when something drastic happens
It takes for a crisis to move us into action

Some people only work hard
when there is an immediate gain
Otherwise they have a constant level
of laziness to maintain
Whatever happened to the values
of hard work and sacrifice
Let's start listening to our elder's advice

There is not enough people

willing to sacrifice for a greater cause

We make them, but yet we break our own laws

I am not pointing the finger at you

because I have made countless mistakes

We got to get it right for heaven's sake

We've all heard the saying that

we can do better if we try

For this reason alone, our harder efforts must multiply

I take the blame for my own hundreds of faults

That's why I flip through self help books

like a world class gymnastic doing somersaults

I have failed so many times so who am I to criticize

My intentions of writing this

was to inspire and mobilize

From the ashes of our burnt bridges

rose this poetical lyricism

Blowing into your eyes

a clear form of constructive self-criticism

IT AIN'T A PRETTY PICTURE

This is a child so why isn't he smiling

There is a deep sadness that this picture is profiling

Inside the frame, my mind wondered

why I didn't have the things I needed

On welfare day, I stuck my hands out and pleaded

A poor single mother on welfare

she did the best that she can

Mama one day this little boy of yours

will grow into a man

Why is the world this way

Poor kids get teased because their parent

gets little or no pay

No where to run because I can't escape myself

Picture my story

as the most painful on your bookshelf

Read about me and the picture will become clear

At times you will see yourself in the mirror

so don't fear

Your mind begins to wonder

as you stare at this boy crying

He looks out at the world as if he is already dying

Yet he knows that he has so much to live for

Only if someone will give him a chance

and open the door

Why can't people see the world as he does

Why can't things be the way he wish they was

You can tell that he is confused

Watching the men that his mother loves,

leave her abused

God please help this child

Ease his hardship and make his life a little more mild

If you look at this picture a little deeper,

you can see hope

A deeper longing for a life

whose fate is not sealed in an envelope

My childhood was never perfect

because I never experienced perfection

All around me,

I saw people going backwards with no direction

Inner city blues in a ghetto full of suffering

is what these eyes see

This is the picture

that is painted in my childhood memory

Still, it wasn't all bad

At times everyone around me seemed glad

That's why I always believed

that things could get better

My mistake was moving too fast as a go-getter

Just when the picture started looking good,

something would mess it up

Drowning out the sound of my voice

with an urgent hiccup

Let my picture do the talking for you

See the world from my point of view

All the pictures don't look good

As an example, picture my childhood

The details as seen in the picture are harsh and gritty

It is a picture that isn't pretty

SOME OF THE GREATEST MINDS ARE IN PRISON

Prison is where you can find a scholar of every kind

The system can lock up a person's body,

but it can't incarcerate their mind

The mind can accomplish what it will

It is stronger than concrete, razor wire, and steel

Through self-rehabilitation

a criminal can turn himself into a citizen

He may have lost in the courtroom,

but by becoming a better man he can win

I was born to be more than just another statistic

So, I had to look at my life

in a way that was more realistic

I am not a model prisoner

because prison doesn't model me

From the beginning,

I was determined to be the best I could be

I was given a prison number

and labeled as a stereotype

I walk the yard every day, but I don't believe the hype

I started reading hundreds of books

History and experience taught me

that not all the men in prison will always be crooks

Some are politicians, accountants,

and professions of every kind

Locked away in prison

is some of the world's greatest minds

They may have committed crimes

that landed them behind bars

Through the pain of their mistakes,

they have healed many of their scars

They went into prison as the problem,

but now they have the solution

Changed men who want to cleanse the world

of its pollution

The smartest people sometimes

do some of the dumbest things

That's how so many great minds

end up in prison wings

Their entrepreneurial spirt was misguided

in a criminal enterprise

In the end, they lost their fortune and freedom

to a prison disguise

Now it's the time to turn things around for the better

The truth of this rhyme is spelled out

in each and every letter

I write this as I sit in prison,

but I am no ordinary fellow

God blessed me with the gift to be a storyteller

So, with my talent, I became an author

and wrote books of every kind

I am a prisoner, but I have a great mind

I succeed against the odds

to claim the greatness that I possess

Now the greatest in me refuses to settle for less

It doesn't stop with the pen and the books that I write

Cause I'm also studying to become a paralegal at night

Then I founded a non-profit organization

for troubled teens headed on a wrong path

I know they can become entrepreneurs

if they don't limit themselves to street math

It doesn't stop there because there is no limit

to the goals that I pursue

There are men/women in prison

who are doing similar things to what I do

It is from the lowest depths

that the greatest of men have risen

Some of the world's greatest minds are in prison

Other Books by Bobby Bostic

Dear Mama: The Life and Struggles of a Single Mother

Generation Misunderstood: Generation Next

Mind Diamonds: Shining on Your Mind

When Life Gives You

lemons:

Make Lemonade

Life Goes on Inside

Prison

Time

Endless Moments

In Prison

Also look for future books, products, and
merchandise by Bobby Bostic.